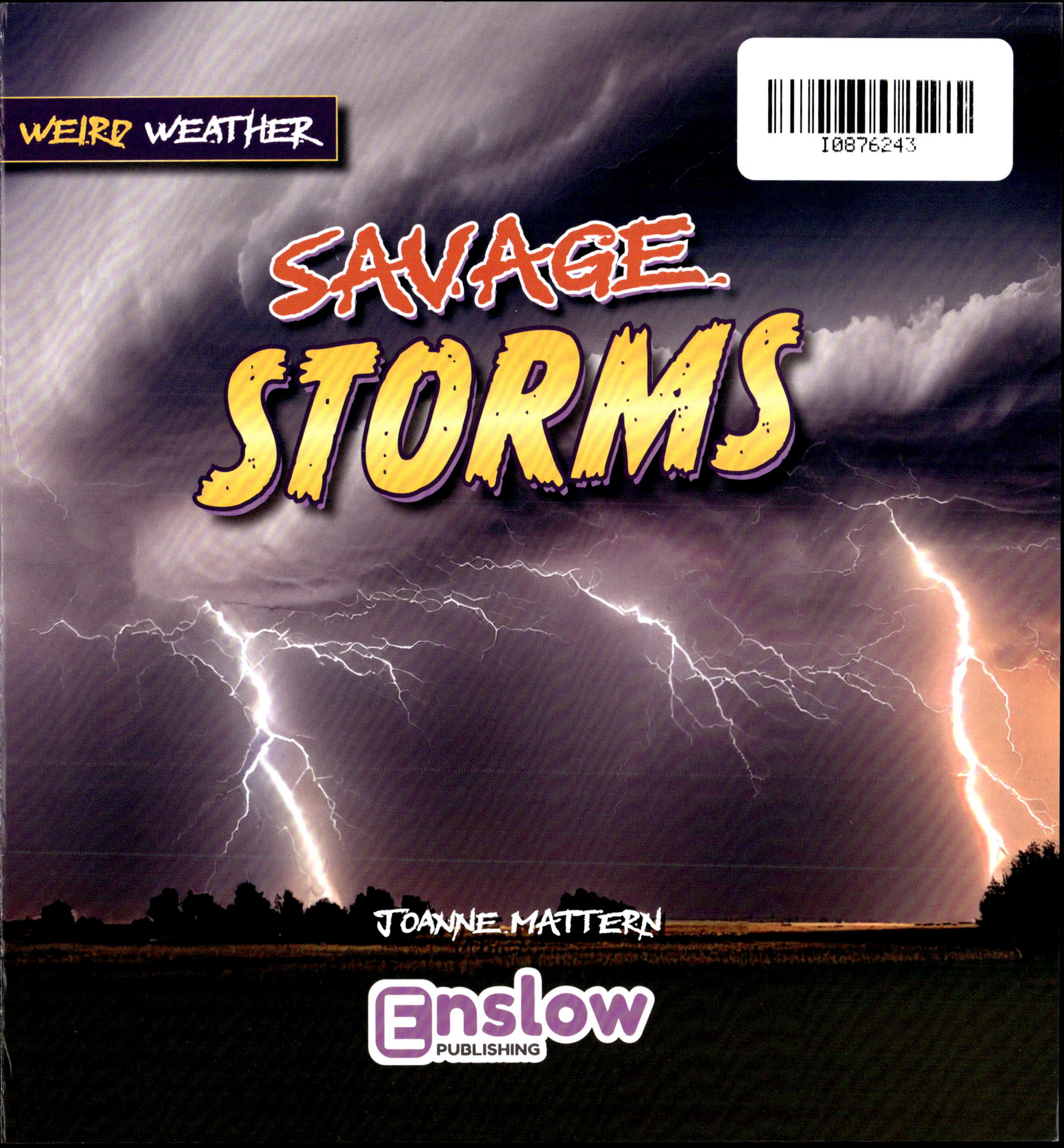

WEIRD WEATHER

SAVAGE STORMS

JOANNE MATTERN

Enslow PUBLISHING

Please visit our website, www.enslow.com. For a free color catalog of all our high-quality books, call toll free 1-800-398-2504 or fax 1-877-980-4454

Published in 2027 by
Enslow Publishing
2544 Clinton Street
Buffalo, NY 14224

Cataloging-in-Publication Data
Names: Mattern, Joanne, 1963-.
Title: Savage storms / Joanne Mattern.
Description: Buffalo, NY : Enslow Publishing, 2027. | Series: Weird weather | Includes glossary.
Identifiers: ISBN 9781978549753 (pbk.) | ISBN 9781978549760 (library bound) | ISBN 9781978549777 (ebook)
Subjects: LCSH: Severe storms--Juvenile literature. | Tornadoes--Juvenile literature. | Hurricanes--Juvenile literature. | Weather--Juvenile literature.
Classification: LCC QC941.3 M375 2027 | DDC 551.55--dc23

Photos Credits: Cover, p.1 ©2022 Xiangyu Han/Shutterstock.com; p.3 and throughout the book ©2020 Cherisha Kay Norman/Shutterstock.com; p.4 ©2020 Dustin Porter/Shutterstock.com; p.4 ©2018 Everett Collection/Shutterstock.com; p.5 ©2018 Everett Collection/Shutterstock.com; p.6, p.7 ©2023 Emre Akkoyun/Shutterstock.com; p.7 ©2018 Everett Collection/Shutterstock.com; p.8 ©2020 Elena11/Shutterstock.com; p.9, p.29 ©2018 NASA images/Shutterstock.com; p.10 ©2024 Dasarath Deka/Shutterstock.com; p.11 ©2020 Alexander Gafarro/Shutterstock.com; p.12 ©2023 Melidis Alexandros/Shutterstock.com; p.13 ©2025 Triff/Shutterstock.com; p.14, p.15, p.29 ©2015 Vasin Lee/Shutterstock.com; p.16, p.28 ©2021 John D Sirlin/Shutterstock.com; p.17 ©2018 RedStarImaging/Shutterstock.com; p.18, p.29 ©2019 John D Sirlin/Shutterstock.com; p.19 ©2015 Chatchawal Kittirojana/Shutterstock.com; p.20 ©2020 justkgoomm/Shutterstock.com; p.21 ©2023 zelvan/Shutterstock.com; p.22, p.23 ©2022 Rejdan/Shutterstock.com; p.24, p.25, p.28 ©2021 Viktor Sergeevich/Shutterstock.com; p.26 ©2022 Anang Fathoni/Shutterstock.com; p.27 ©2025 Ann Stryzhekin/Shutterstock.com

Printed in China

CPSIA compliance information: Batch #QSENS27: For further information, contact Enslow Publishing, New York, New York, at 1-800-398-2504.

TABLE OF CONTENTS

Words in the glossary appear in **bold** type the first time they are used in the text.

It was a stormy day in Galveston, Texas. People had heard that a big storm was crossing the Gulf of America. But no one was worried. Weather **forecasters** did not expect it to hit the city.

The forecasters were wrong. On September 8, 1900, one of the deadliest storms ever hit Galveston. The damage was unbelievable. Winds of more than 130 miles (209 kilometers) per hour smashed houses and trees. Sixteen-foot (five-meter) waves flooded the city. Almost every building was damaged or destroyed.

The Galveston hurricane killed as many as 12,000 people. Some bodies were never found. It is the deadliest natural disaster to ever hit the United States.

Why did so many people die in the Galveston hurricane? Weather forecasters did not have the tools to predict the storm. Also, Galveston was in an area that often flooded. Hurricanes are one of the most powerful and deadly storms on Earth. The people of Galveston had no chance against such a savage storm.

A HORRIBLE NIGHT

One writer who survived the Galveston hurricane said it was "a tempest so terrible that no words can adequately describe its intensity."

A HURRICANE BEGINS

Hurricanes form over the ocean. They begin when rain and thunderstorms circle around an area of low air pressure.

In certain conditions, warm air over the ocean rises in a spiral. As the air rises, it cools and **condenses** into storm clouds. More warm air rises, getting stronger and faster. If winds reach 74 miles (119 kilometers) per hour, the storm is called a hurricane.

The winds spin around a calm area in the middle of the storm. This area is called the eye. The eye is calm. But the eyewall surrounding it is not. The eyewall is where the highest winds and heaviest rain happen.

WHAT'S IN A NAME?

What's the difference between a hurricane, a typhoon, and a cyclone? Nothing! Storms in the southern Pacific and Indian Oceans are called cyclones. Storms in the western Pacific are called typhoons. Hurricanes form in the northern Pacific and Atlantic Oceans.

DANGER IN ALL DIRECTIONS

Hurricanes are deadly because they create a triple punch: wind, flooding, and storm surges. High winds blow down trees and power lines. Heavy rain can cause flooding.

A storm surge happens when hurricane winds push water onto the shore. The huge waves cause flooding, but that's not all! The weight of the pounding waves can destroy docks, roads, houses, and beaches.

TOP SPEEDS

Hurricane winds are measured by the Saffir-Simpson Hurricane Wind Scale. A Category 1 hurricane has wind speeds of 74 to 95 miles (119 to 153 kilometers) per hour. A Category 5 hurricane has winds of 157 miles (253 kilometers) per hour or more!

BIG BANGS, BRIGHT LIGHTS

Thunderstorms form when warm, wet air quickly rises into cooler, **unstable** air above. The water **vapor** in the air condenses and forms a cloud. As the cloud grows taller, that means a storm is coming.

The inside of a thundercloud is a **violent** place. As air moves around, it creates an electric charge. In time, that charge is so strong, the electricity is released as a lightning bolt.

Thunder and lightning go together. As the electricity moves through the air, it creates a shock wave. That is the sound we call thunder.

STORMY WEATHER

There are about 16 million thunderstorms every year. About 100,000 of them happen in the United States.

COUNT IT DOWN

Light travels faster than sound. That means you will see lightning before you hear its thunder. To figure out how far away the lightning is, count the number of seconds between them. Then, divide that number by five. The answer is the number of miles you are from the lightning.

Thunder is scary and loud, but it can't hurt you. It's just noise. But lightning can be very dangerous. More than 20 people in the United States are killed by lightning every year. Even more are injured. If you hear thunder or see lightning, get inside and stay safe.

SUPER SAVAGE CELLS

Not all thunderstorms are the same. If you ever see a tall, anvil-shaped cloud that is spinning, run for cover. You are looking at a supercell.

Supercells are filled with violent winds. These winds are moving up and around. That spinning motion causes bad storms. Supercells can create heavy rain and hail. They can even cause tornadoes. These storms can last for hours.

Supercells can happen anywhere in the world. But they are most common in the central part of the United States.

WHIRLING WINDS

*The spinning wind in a supercell is called a **mesocyclone**.*

LET'S GET WET

Savage storms can produce a lot of rain. A thunderstorm might last a few minutes. A hurricane might last a few days. But some weather systems last for months! That's what happens with a monsoon.

A monsoon is caused by changing winds. These winds pull **moisture** from the ocean and move it onto land. Monsoons are weather patterns, not storms. But they create stormy conditions.

Monsoons are most common in India and other parts of Asia. The southwestern part of the United States has a monsoon season too.

HELPFUL STORMS

Monsoons aren't all bad! Monsoon rains help ***replenish*** *water supplies. They also provide water for crops.*

SPINNING STORMS

Savage storms don't always bring rain. One type brings snow. Lots of snow! This storm is called a nor'easter.

Nor'easters are most common along the eastern coast of the United States. They get their name from the way the wind blows. A nor'easter's winds blow from—you guessed it!—the northeast.

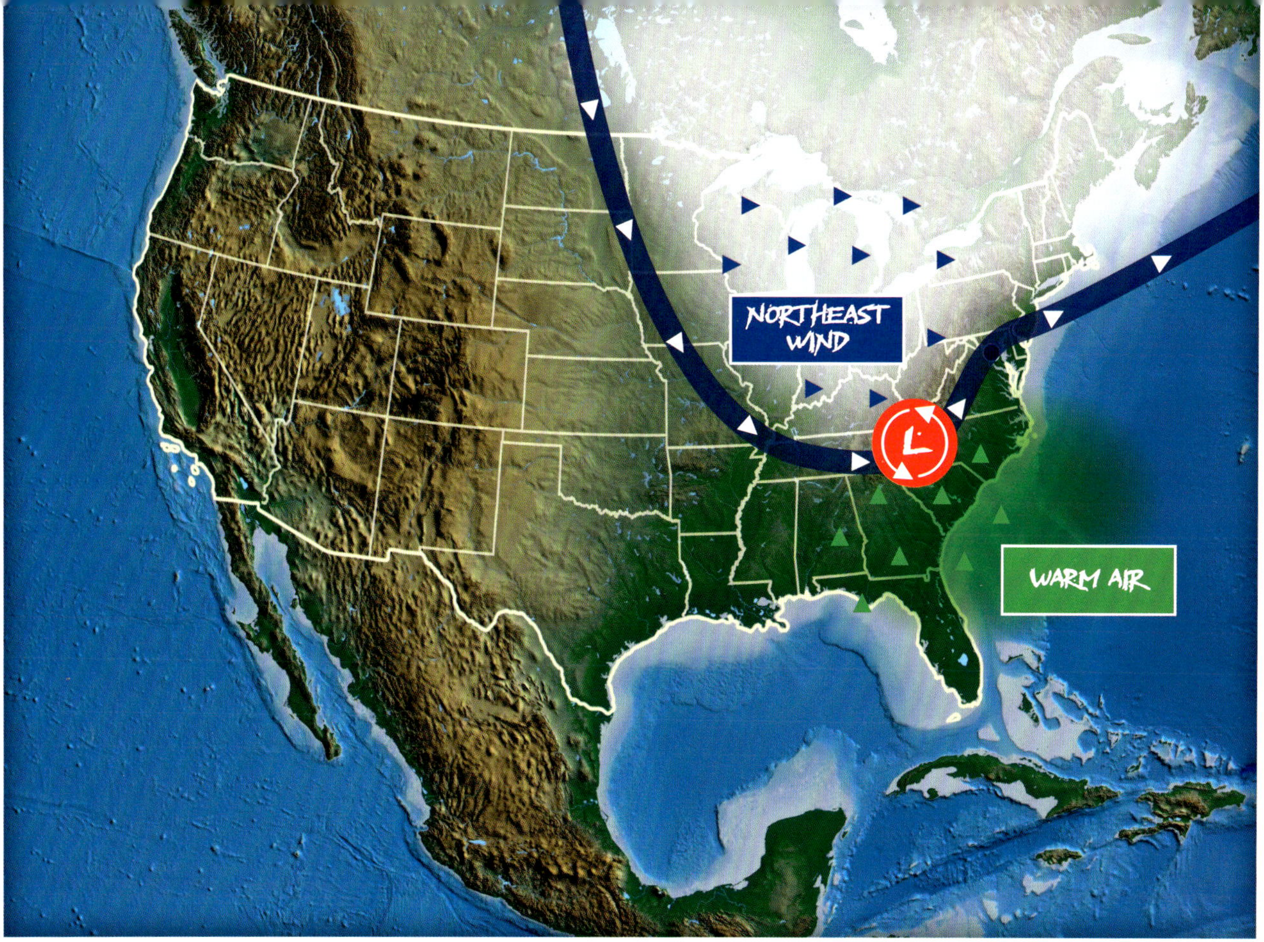

In the winter, cold air flows south and east from Canada. Warm air flows north from the Gulf of America. When these **air masses** hit each other, a savage storm can happen.

A nor'easter can strike any time of year. But most happen between September and April. At that time of year, the air is often cold enough to create snow. And a nor'easter can make lots of it!

The Blizzard of 1888 dumped up to 55 inches (1.4 meters) of snow in some parts of the eastern United States. The wind blew 85 miles (137 kilometers) per hour. More than 400 people died. So did thousands of animals.

The storm hit New York City hard. Thousands of people were stranded on overhead trains. Thousands more had to find shelter in hotels when they couldn't get home. People were stuck for days!

March 1993 saw another powerful nor'easter. The storm lasted for three days. It brought heavy snow, rain, and wind to most of the eastern U.S. More than 130 million people were affected. At one point, every airport from Canada to Georgia was closed.

It was called "The Storm of the Century." Even Southern cities, which don't get much snow, felt the storm's power. Birmingham, Alabama, had six-foot (1.8-meter) snowdrifts. A mountain in Tennessee recorded 56 inches (1.4 meters) of snow. That's one savage storm!

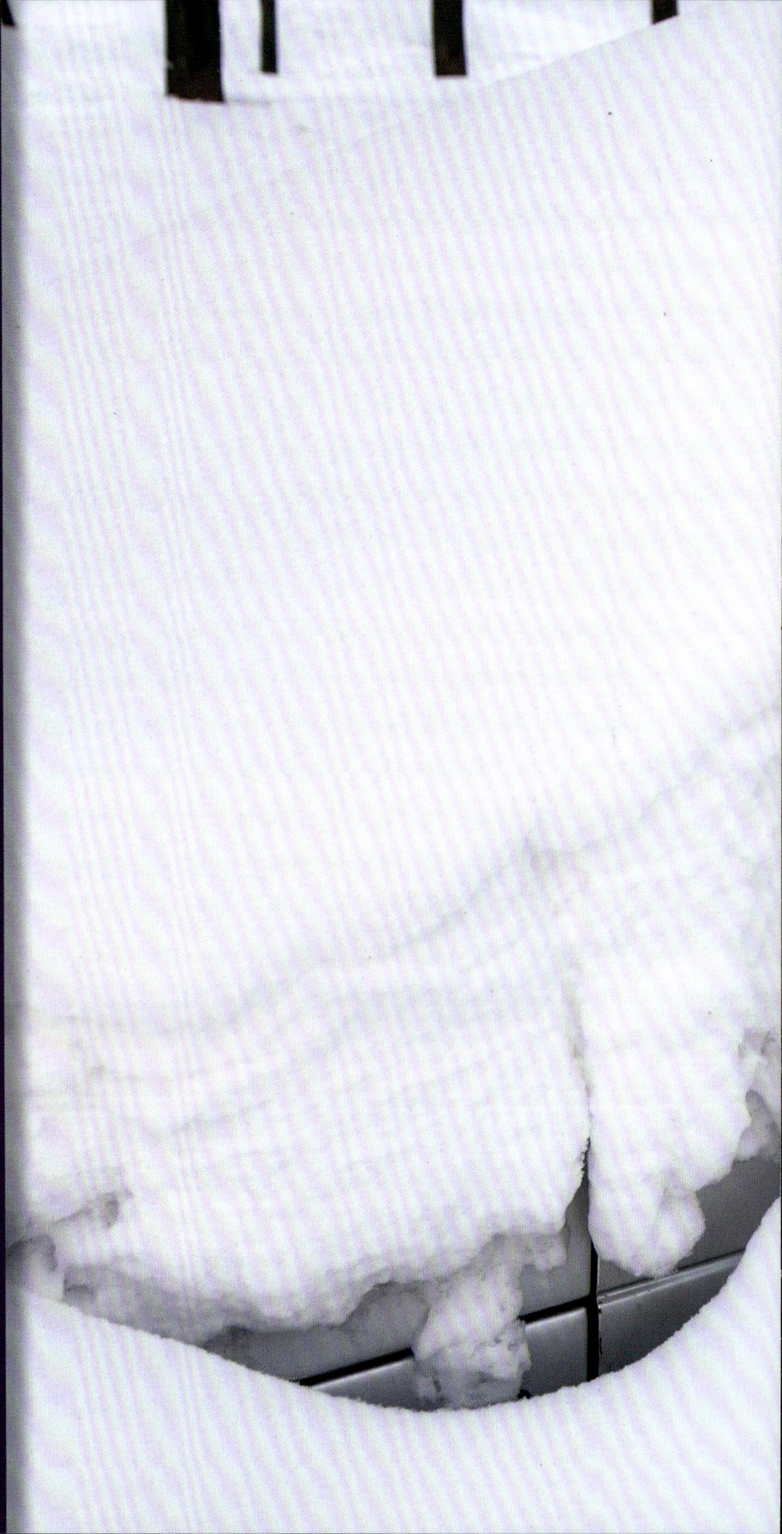

RAINING CATS AND DOGS?

No one has ever seen it rain cats and dogs. But other animals have rained from the sky! This event is more common than you think.

"Animal rains" happen when a storm passes over a lake or other body of water. The strong winds can suck fish, frogs, and other small animals out of the water. Then, the storm drops them on land. Imagine seeing animals falling from the sky! That kind of storm sure is savage for the poor creatures involved.

BLOWN OFF COURSE

A powerful storm can also blow birds off course. Many people have reported seeing shorebirds far from the water during a hurricane. The winds carried the birds far from home.

WHAT AM I?

Can you guess what type of savage storm is shown in each photo? Look closely at these images and use the clues to help you figure it out. Then, check your answers below. How many did you get right?

1

My cold, swirling air likes to set big snow records. What am I?

2

Wind, rain, hail—I've got it all. But you'd better take shelter when I come to town. What am I?

3

My bright lights and energy might give you the shock of your life if you get too close. What am I?

4

I put the rain in the rainy season, but my wet weather helps crops grow. What am I?

5

I've got my "eye" on you! But you'd better keep an eye out for my heavy rain and high winds. What am I?

1. nor'easter; 2. supercell; 3. lightning; 4. monsoon; 5. hurricane

GLOSSARY

air masses (air mas-siz): groupings of air in the atmosphere that have about the same temperature and amount of moisture

condenses (kun-DEN-sez): changes from a gas to a liquid

forecasters (FOR-kas-turz): people who predict something

mesocyclone (mez-oh-SY-klone): the spinning winds in a thundercloud

moisture (MOYS-chur): dampness

replenish (ree-PLEN-ish): to refill

unstable (uhn-STAY-buhl): not steady; likely to change

vapor (VAY-pur): a gas formed from something that is usually a liquid or solid at normal temperatures

violent (VY-uh-lent): strong and destructive

FACT CHECK

1. The center of a hurricane is called the __________.
   a. cyclone b. eye c. surge
2. You hear thunder __________ you see lightning.
   a. after b. before c. at the same time
3. Most nor'easters happen in the __________.
   a. summer b. spring c. winter

Answers: 1. b, 2. a, 3. c

FURTHER READING

Cappucci, Matthew. *Extreme Weather for Kids.* Quarry Books, 2024.
Kentner, Julie. *Thunderstorms.* The Child's World, Inc., 2025.
Mattern, Joanne. *The Worst Hurricanes on Record.* Mitchell Lane Publishers, 2025.

ON THE INTERNET

Hurricanes
https://kids.nationalgeographic.com/science/article/hurricane
This National Geographic Kids article explains how hurricanes form and the destruction they can cause.

Thunderstorms
www.weatherwizkids.com/weather/thunderstorms/#google_vignette
This page features descriptions, facts, and photos of the many different types of thunderstorms.

Publisher's note to educators and parents: Our editors have carefully reviewed these websites to ensure that they are suitable for students. Many websites change frequently, however, and we cannot guarantee that a site's future contents will continue to meet our high standards of quality and educational value. Be advised that students should be closely supervised whenever they access the internet.

INDEX

ABOUT THE AUTHOR

Joanne Mattern is the author of many books for children on a variety of subjects, including science, history, and biography. She loves writing about and experiencing weird weather events! Joanne loves to learn about people, places, and events and bring historical figures to life for today's readers. She lives in New York State with her family.